LOST AND FOUND

JOHN MALAM

QEB Publishing

This edition published by Scholastic Inc.,
557 Broadway, New York, NY 10012,
by arrangement with
QEB Publishing, Inc.,
3 Wrigley, Suite A,
Irvine, CA 92618

Project Editor Carey Scott
Designer Stefan Morris Design
Illustrations The Art Agency
and MW Digital Graphics
Picture Researcher Maria Joannou

Distributed by Scholastic Canada Ltd, Markham, Ontario

A CIP record for this book is available from the Library of Congress.

Printed in Guangdong, China
10 9 8 7 6 5 4 3 2 1

ISBN 978-0-545-38762-0

Picture credits

Key: t=top, b=bottom, r=right, l=left, c=center
Alamy Images Ancient Art & Architecture Collection Ltd 5tl, Steve Davey Photography 9b, Images David Lyons 29t, Lou McGill 29b; The Art Agency Ian Jackson 10b, 15, 19b, 28b, 32b, 42b, 47b; Corbis Eddie Keogh/Reuters 37, Paul Souders 40t, Jason Hawkes Jim Hollander/EPA 45br, Adam Woolfitt 46b, Bettmann 49b, Ian Jackson 60b, 57b; Bridgeman Art Library Giraudon 21r, Iraq Museum, Collection of the New-York Historical Society, USA 33t, Giraudon 59b; Corbis Robert Harding World Imagery 6bl, Sandro Vannini 7t, 8b, Nathan Benn 11t, The Gallery Collection 14b, Fine Art 16t, Adam Woolfitt 3, Michael DeFreitas/Robert Harding World Imagery 22b, Reuters Photographer/Reuters 23t, Roger Ressmeyer 27b, Nathan Benn/Ottochrome 29, Adam Woolfitt 31t, John Garrett 31b; DK Images Richard Bonson 38b, Eddie Keogh/Reuters 51, Paul Souders 55t, Jim Hollander/EPA 63br, Mimmo Jodice 56b, Richard Bonson 52b; Getty Images Gallo Images/Mike Copeland 5tr, Hulton Archive 8t, Stone/Michael Melford 9t, Gallo Images/Danita Delimont 26b, The British Library 22t, The Picture Desk Art Archive/Bibliothèque des Arts Décoratifs Paris/Gianni Dagli Orti 24b, 25b, AFP Photo/Nikolay Doychinov 36bl, National Geographic/O. Louis Mazzatenta 37b, ChinaFotoPress 40–41b, AFP/Norbert Millauer 41t, Photolibrary Michael Krabs 37t, AFP Photo/ Nikolay Doychinov 50bl, National Geographic/O. Louis Mazzatenta 53b, ChinaFotoPress 54-55b, AFP/Norbert Millauer 55t, AFP/Menahem Kahana 62bl, National Geographic 62-63, AFP/Mario Laporta 57t, Roger Viollet 58br; Photolibrary Michael Krabs 53t; Photoshot World Illustrated 49t; Rex Features Alinari 36tr; The Manchester Museum Barbara Heller 19t; The Picture Desk Art Archive/Archaeological Museum Volos/Gianni Dagli Orti 5b, Art Archive/Genius of China Exhibition 20, Art Archive/Musée du Louvre Paris/Gianni Dagli Orti 58t, 58bl, 59t, 59c; Rex Features Brian Harris 17b, Alinari 50tr; Shutterstock Dudarev Mikhail 4, Bragin Alexey 2l I.T 7b, Bragin Peter Zaharov 26t, Jule_Berlin 30, Steffen Foerster Photography 34t, Damian Gil 35; Topham Picturepoint The Image Works 23b, Alinari 27t, The Granger Collection 33b, 34b, Denisart 38–39 (background); Topham Picturepoint 39b, 48-49b, The British Library 38tl, 48t, Denisart 54–55 (background), Denisart 62–63 (background), Ella's Design 61t; Topham Picturepoint 16b, Museum of London 15tl, The Granger Collection 17t, 18b, FotoWare FotoStation 21l, 55b, The British Library 52tl, The Granger Collection 61b. All maps by Mark Walker at MW Digital Graphics 6t, 14t, 18t.

CONTENTS

WHAT IS A LOST TOMB?

A tomb is a special place where the remains of a dead person are buried. It is meant to be a place where the person can rest in peace forever. Some tombs are built above ground so everyone can see them. Other tombs are buried deep underground, or cut out of the side of a mountain.

▼ The Ancient Egyptians built the pyramids as tombs for their rulers, but tomb raiders broke into most of them and stole the treasures hidden inside.

Inside Tombs

For ancient people, tombs were the place where the dead person began the life after death, so they were filled with objects, known as grave goods, for the person to use in the afterlife.

The tombs of some kings, emperors, and other rulers also contained the bodies of ordinary people. They were the servants of the ruler who had been sacrificed, or deliberately killed, so they could serve and protect their leader in the afterlife.

◂ These decorated containers, called canopic jars, were used to hold body parts of the dead.

▲ Burial mounds, such as this one, are tombs that were built in prehistoric times in Europe.

Lost to the World

After a while, people stopped visiting the tombs. The dead people buried inside were forgotten, and the tombs became lost. Tomb raiders discovered some and stole the treasures inside them, but many tombs and their hidden treasures have stayed buried for hundreds or thousands of years.

Grave Goods

This is the grave of an ordinary person, containing a few cooking pots for him or her to use in the afterlife. The tombs of important people have contained thousands of valuable objects, including chariots and ships. But even simple grave goods are valuable to archeologists.

LOST: EGYPTIAN PHARAOH

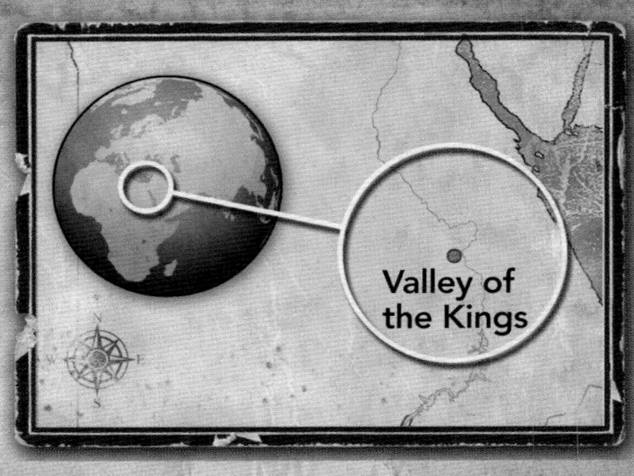

Location: Valley of the Kings, Egypt
Date: around 1323 BC

Tutankhamun became the pharaoh, which means king, of Egypt when he was nine years old. But his reign was short because he died when he was just 19 years old.

▶ In this painting, Tutankhamun is shown in his chariot, firing arrows at his enemies during one of the wars of Ancient Egypt.

Burying a Mummy

Because Tutankhamun died so young, his royal tomb was not yet ready for him. Instead of a huge tomb for a king, his tomb was meant for an ordinary person and was small. It had four rooms, which were cut into the rock in the side of a valley.

Royal servants mummified Tutankhamun's body to preserve it. They placed a golden death mask over the mummy's head and shoulders. Then they put the mummy into a nest of three coffins, one inside the other, and lowered the coffin nest into a fourth coffin made of stone. They filled the tomb with thousands of objects for the king to use in the afterlife.

◀ This gold figure of Tutankhamun shows the king wearing a crown of Egypt and holding a crook and flail—symbols of the Egyptian pharaohs.

Resting in Peace

About 200 years later, a tomb for the new pharaoh was built above Tutankhamun's. As the builders worked, they sent loose rocks tumbling down the cliff on top of Tutankhamun's tomb, making it even harder to find.

Valley of the Kings

The valley where Tutankhamun was buried is known as the Valley of the Kings. Over around 500 years, more than 60 tombs for pharaohs and nobles were dug there. Some were built deep into the cliffs and had many rooms, but others, such as Tutankhamun's, were much smaller. Almost all the tombs were raided in ancient times.

FOUND: TUTANKHAMUN'S TOMB

▲ Howard Carter carefully removes a layer of sticky resin from Tutankhamun's mummy.

▼ This necklace, with its sacred design, was found on Tutankhamun's mummy.

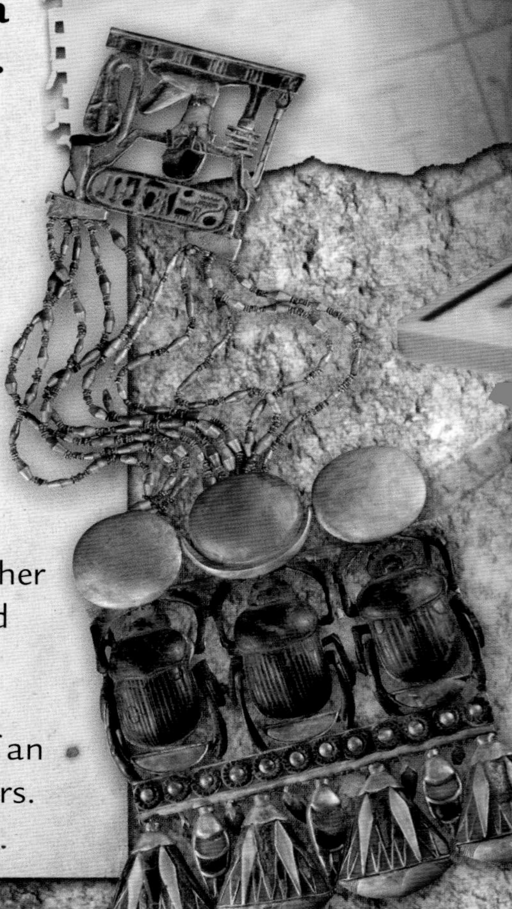

Could there be a lost tomb in the Valley of the Kings, untouched by thieves and still full of treasure? An English archeologist, Howard Carter, was convinced there was a tomb belonging to Tutankhamun.

Long Search

In 1922, after five years searching the Valley of the Kings, Carter's luck finally changed. As his workers cleared rubble, a flight of 12 steps going down into the ground was revealed. At the foot of the steps was the door to a tomb, and on the door was the name Tutankhamun.

On the other side of the door was a short passageway, and at the end of that was another door. Carter made a hole through the second door. He pushed a candle into the darkness beyond and saw the glint of gold. It was an incredible sight—the treasures in the tomb of an Ancient Egyptian pharaoh, lost for 3,300 years.

The Death Mask

Tutankhamun's death mask was placed over the head of the pharaoh's mummy. It was made from gold inlaid with blue glass and semiprecious stones. The mask shows the pharaoh wearing a headcloth over his shoulders. He has a royal vulture and cobra on his forehead and a decorative beard on his chin.

▼ Today, Tutankhamun's mummy still lies in its inmost coffin inside his tomb.

FACT FILE

There were so many precious objects inside Tutankhamun's tomb that it took 10 years to pack and remove them all.

LOST: SOUTH AMERICAN LORD

Long ago, Peru was home to the Moche people. They buried their dead inside huge burial mounds that looked like flat-topped pyramids. They made these mounds from millions of mud bricks.

Location: Sipán, Peru
Date: around 700 AD

Magnificent Burial

Almost 2,000 years ago, a Moche ruler, known today as the Lord of Sipán, died. His body was buried with precious objects, such as gold and copper headdresses and fans made from feathers.

Servants wrapped his body and all these grave goods in three layers of colorful cloth and fitted the bundle inside a large wooden coffin. They lowered the coffin into a burial chamber, dug deep into the center of a mud brick pyramid.

◀ The Lord of Sipán is shown here dressed in royal costume with two attendants.

▲ These Moche models of fierce jaguars are actually bottles. Liquid was poured from their mouths.

Servant Sacrifices

Three men and two women were buried with the Lord of Sipán. They were sacrifices—people who had served him when he was alive, and who were killed so they could carry on working for him in the life after death.

Burial Mounds

When they were new, the Moche burial mounds had flat tops. These were used as platforms for building temples and for performing ceremonies. There were long, sloping ramps for people to reach the platforms. The whole structure was made of mud bricks, baked hard by the sun.

FOUND: LORD OF SIPÁN'S TOMB

▲ Inside the shaft dug by tomb raiders, archeologists uncover the tomb of the Lord of Sipán.

▶ The Lord of Sipán lies in the center of his grave, surrounded by four faithful servants.

In the 1980s, tomb raiders began digging into one of the mounds at Sipán. When police officers searched their homes, they found a haul of treasure. Archeologist Walter Alva was called in.

Police Patrol

Alva was amazed at the incredible gold objects, and he wondered what else might be discovered. The police set up patrols to keep the villagers away so that Alva could begin excavating.

Alva knew the mound probably contained many tombs and the raiders had found just one. He spotted a place they had missed, and as he dug away the crumbled remains of ancient mud brick, he revealed the outline of a coffin, untouched by the thieves. Nothing like it had ever been found before. Alva named the dead man the Lord of Sipán, and his tomb is the richest ever found in South America.

FACT FILE

As well as his servants, the Lord of Sipán's tomb contained the body of a dog. It was probably his favorite pet.

Gold Pectoral

The Lord of Sipán was buried with 11 gold pectorals, or chest ornaments, on his body. They were probably part of his ceremonial jewelry. This pectoral is in the shape of an octopus and has a human head.

LOST: ANGLO-SAXON KING

England was once divided into several kingdoms, and each was ruled by a powerful king. The eastern part of the country belonged to the kingdom of the East Angles, whose first king was Redwald.

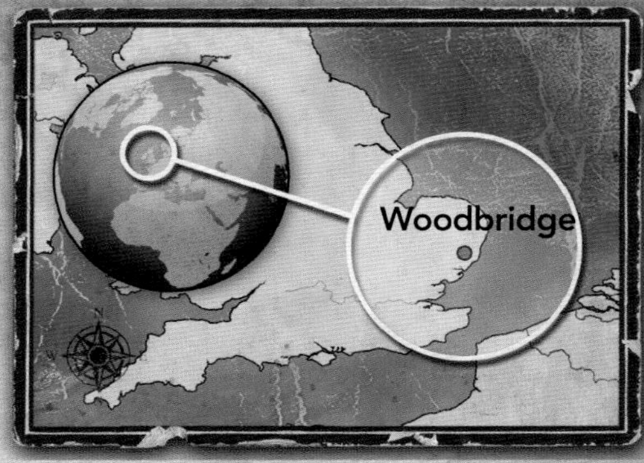

Location: near Woodbridge, England
Date: around 625 AD

Battles of Kingdoms

The kingdoms fought one another and raided each other's territory. In one battle, fought in 616 AD, King Redwald defeated the rival king of Northumbria. About nine years later, King Redwald died. As a great warrior and king, he would have been laid to rest in a grand tomb.

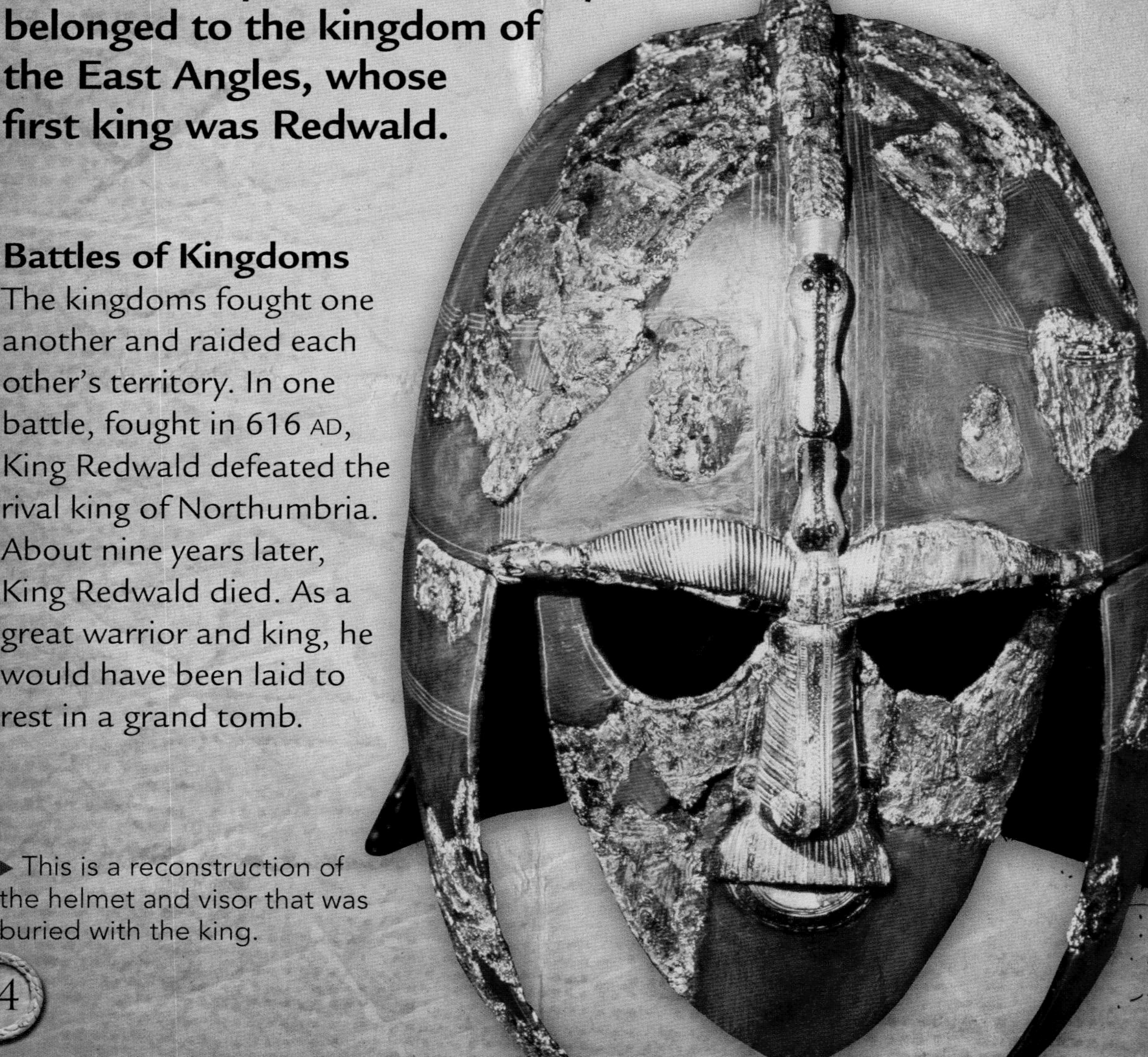

▸ This is a reconstruction of the helmet and visor that was buried with the king.

Anglo-Saxon Swords

Swords were the main weapons for Anglo-Saxon warriors. The blades were made of iron which was sharpened along both edges. The finest swords had gold fittings decorated with red garnets (semiprecious stones). After a battle, the victors stripped these fittings from the swords of the defeated warriors, as a way of showing their triumph. Those warriors who died peacefully were often buried with their swords.

▼ Experts think that the body of King Redwald and his grave goods were placed inside a wooden chamber within the ship.

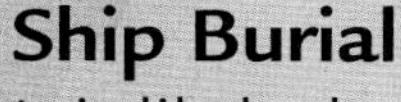

Ship Burial

It is likely that King Redwald was buried in a wooden ship dragged up onto the land, as were other rulers of the time from northern Europe. Everything a warrior king might need in the next life would have been placed around his body. Then servants would have covered the ship in a huge mound of earth.

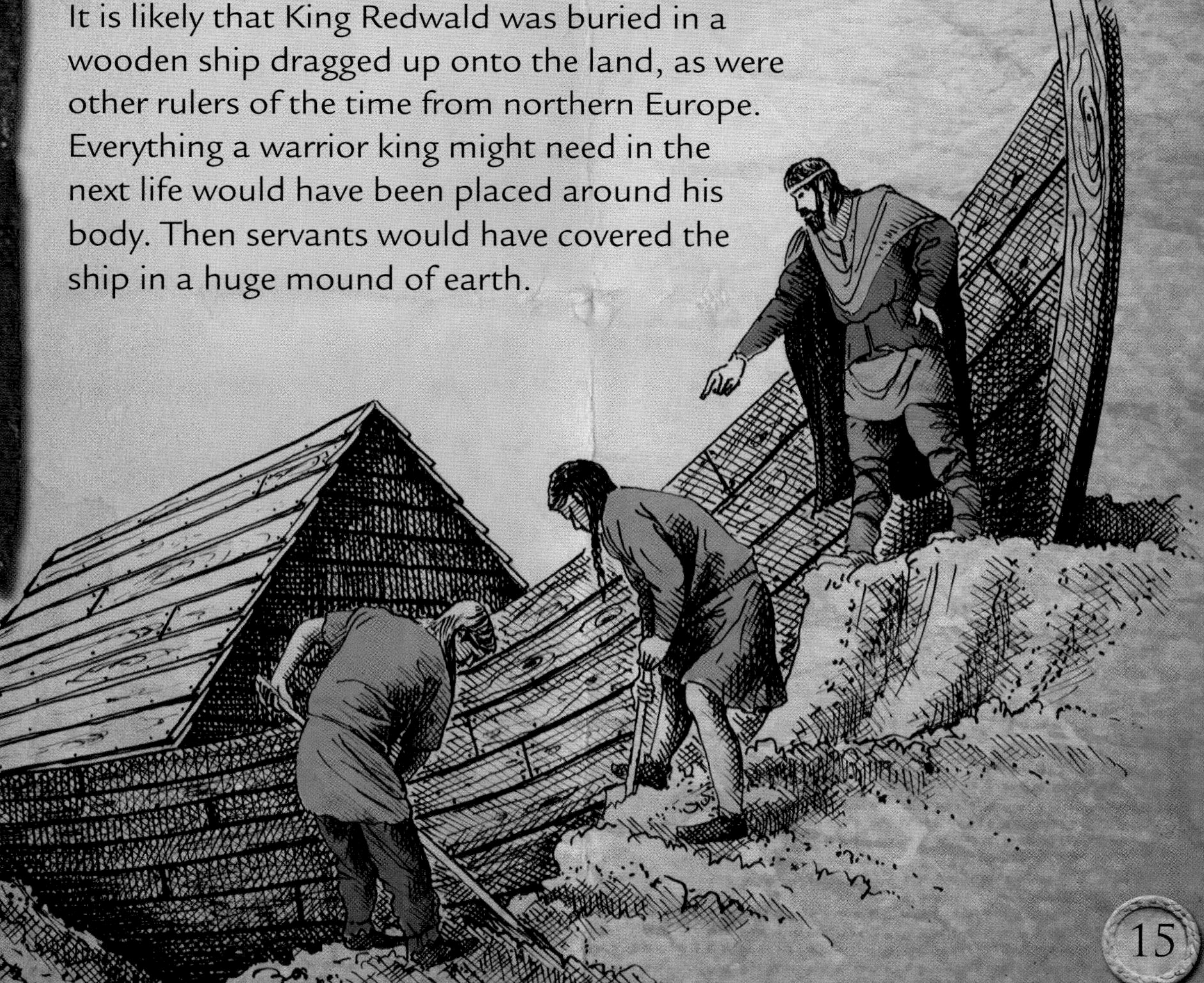

FOUND:
KING REDWALD'S TOMB?

In 1938, archeologist Basil Brown excavated some mysterious mounds at Sutton Hoo, in the east of England. At first, all he could find inside them were large iron nails.

Ancient Longship

They were the type of nails used to hold wooden planks together on ancient ships. As Brown cleared away the sandy earth, he saw that the nails were in lines. Slowly, the impression of an ancient ship was revealed. The wood had rotted away, but the lines of nails showed where the planks had once been.

In the center of the ship was a burial chamber, untouched by tomb raiders. Inside were weapons and armor, coins and jewelry, and silver and bronze bowls. All that was missing was a body, which the acidic soil had dissolved—bones and all. Experts cannot be certain who was buried in the Sutton Hoo ship, but they believe it was Redwald, king of the East Angles.

► It is possible King Redwald himself owned this solid gold belt clasp.

▼ This small, decorated bronze plaque would have been fixed to the side of a large jug.

▲ The ghostly impression of the Anglo-Saxon ship found in the sandy earth at Sutton Hoo.

FACT FILE

The Sutton Hoo ship did not have a sail. It was powered by 40 strong men using oars.

Sutton Hoo Burial Ground

There are around 20 burial mounds at Sutton Hoo, probably all the graves of important people. But Sutton Hoo is also a burial place for people who died violently, from hanging or beheading. These people were buried in ordinary graves near the burial mounds.

LOST: HAN PRINCE

Ancient China was divided into different states, ruled by powerful families, or dynasties. One of the strongest was the Han Dynasty, which controlled a large area in the west of China.

Location: Lingshan, Mancheng County, southwest China
Date: 113 B.C.E.

Age of Prosperity

The Han Dynasty lasted for around 400 years, during which time China prospered. The population increased, the arts flourished, and new things were invented, such as paper and the wheelbarrow. A major trade route was set up linking China with people far to the west. In 113 B.C.E. Prince Liu Sheng, the son of the emperor of China, died.

◀ This painting shows the Han Dynasty army on the move.

The Magic of Jade

Jade is a hard, smooth stone, usually green or white. It has always been highly valued in China because people believed it had magical powers. They thought jade would protect and preserve the body.

Tomb of Treasures

A tomb was built for the prince inside a mountain. A long passageway was dug into it and, at the end, a large tomb was carved out of the solid rock. The tomb was filled with 2,700 grave goods—chariots, silks, and objects made of jade, gold, and silver.

The prince himself was dressed top to toe in a burial suit made from almost 2,500 pieces of jade. This incredible suit was designed to protect Liu Sheng's body forever.

▼ Objects for Prince Liu Sheng to use in the afterlife filled the passageway that led to his burial chamber.

FOUND: LIU SHENG'S TOMB

The mountain at Lingshan, in southwest China, kept its secret for more than 2,000 years, until 1968.

Discovered at Last

In that year, Chinese soldiers climbed the mountain and went inside what they thought was a cave. They came across bronze, jade, and clayware objects. Soon it became clear the soldiers had stumbled across a huge tomb dug deep into the mountain.

The tomb had several rooms. On either side of the entrance were storerooms crammed with objects. At the end of the passageway was a large room filled with bronze objects and figures of servants. A marble door led into a smaller room. Inside that room was a heap of jade squares, which seemed to be in the shape of a human body.

Jade Suit Rebuilt

Inscriptions on grave goods said that this was the tomb of Prince Liu Sheng. His body had rotted away long ago, but archeologists determined that the jade squares were the remains of his burial suit. The suit was taken to a museum, where experts put it back together until it seemed as though Prince Liu Sheng was inside it once more.

▼ Prince Liu Sheng's jade suit may have taken ten years to make. It would have been started while he was still alive.

Incense Burner

Prince Liu Sheng was buried with this incense burner, made in the shape of a mountain. As the incense burned, sweet-smelling smoke rose out of holes in the container, like mist covering a mountain. Incense was burned to please the gods, who were thought to like its smell.

FACT FILE

The jade pieces that make up the burial suits of Prince Liu Sheng and his wife, Lady Dou Wan, were sewn together with gold wire.

WHAT IS A LOST CITY?

It may seem hard to believe, but cities and towns have vanished without a trace. Natural disasters, such as volcanoes and floods, are usually the reason people abandon their cities for good.

When They Were Lost

There are lost cities all over the world. Some, such as Mohenjo-daro, Pakistan, and Pompeii, Italy, were lost thousands of years ago. Others, such as Machu Picchu, the famous Lost City of the Incas in Peru, were lived in more recently.

▼ In 1692, a powerful earthquake struck the island of Jamaica. The town of Port Royal was destroyed, and most of it was plunged to the bottom of the ocean.

▼ Machu Picchu was built by the Inca people in the 1400s, but they soon abandoned it—no one knows why. The city was found in 1911.

▲ Part of the Ancient Egyptian city of Alexandria now lies beneath the Mediterranean Sea. Divers have recovered Ancient Egyptian and Roman statues from the seabed.

Back in Time

Frozen in time, lost cities are filled with clues about what really happened in history. For archeologists, they are a chance to go back in time and find out about the people who lived, worked, and died in them. Many lost cities have now become tourist attractions.

Ghost Towns

Unlike lost cities, ghost towns, such as Bodie, California, have not been forgotten. What ghost towns have in common with lost cities is that no one lives in them anymore. Bodie was a gold mining town in 1859, but when its last mine was closed in 1942, Bodie became a ghost town.

LOST: A ROMAN TOWN

The 20,000 Romans whose home was Pompeii lived in the shadow of a volcano—Mount Vesuvius. In the year 79 AD, the volcano awoke.

Location: Pompeii, Italy.
Date: August 24, 79 AD

Cloud of Doom

On August 20, a small earthquake rocked the town and the people of Pompeii became afraid. Four days later, a dirty gray cloud rose from the summit of the oddly shaped hill. Only then did the townspeople realize that Vesuvius was a volcano and it was waking up after a long, long sleep.

All that day, ash fell from the cloud, covering Pompeii's streets. Most people fled, but around 2,000 stayed in the city. Late that night, tremors shook the ground and lightning flashed through the sky.

▲ A couple collecting water from a street fountain and a customer buying a snack at a food bar, before the eruption.

Other Lost Towns

Pompeii was not the only town destroyed when Vesuvius erupted. The nearby towns of Stabiae and Oplontis were also buried by ash, and Herculaneum was lost beneath a deep layer of mud. In the countryside around the volcano, most of the farms and villas were destroyed.

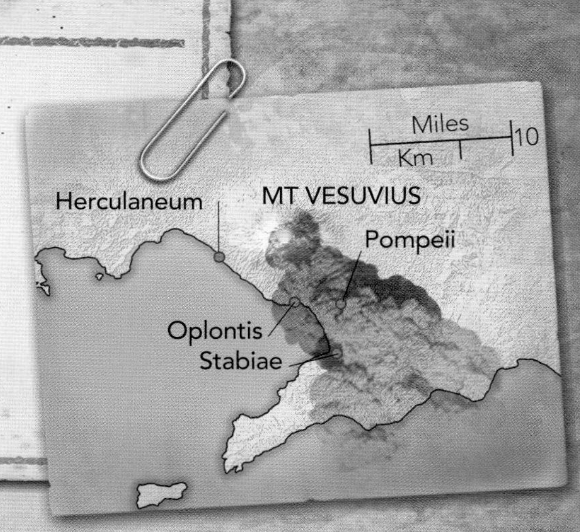

Pompeii Buried

The next day, August 25, torrents of red-hot ash, pumice, and rock spouted from Vesuvius, reaching the town in minutes and smothering it. Pompeii was buried and had become a lost city.

▼ When Vesuvius erupted, day turned to night. People who stayed in their homes had no chance.

FOUND:
POMPEII

▲ A Pompeii street, once littered with rotting vegetables, animal dung, and other garbage.

As the centuries passed, Pompeii became a distant memory. Even its name was forgotten. Local people called it *la cività*, meaning "the city."

Name Returned

In the 1740s, treasure hunters started digging into *la cività* in search of statues and other valuables to sell to wealthy collectors. In 1763, one treasure hunter found a stone with Latin writing on it that solved the mystery of the city's real name. The stone said the city was called Pompeii.

Plaster People

Excavator Giuseppe Fiorelli has made plaster casts of the dips left in the volcanic ash by decomposed bodies. Although the actual bodies and skeletons rotted away long ago, their ghostly outlines remained. So today we can see the bodies of people exactly as they were at the moment of death, more than 2,000 years ago.

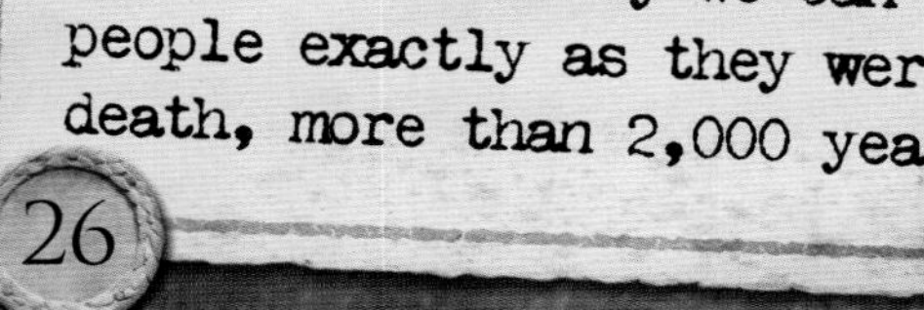

Brought Back to Life

Today, excavators have cleared much of the ash that covered the city, and the Roman streets and buildings have come back to life. Pompeii is a complete Roman city that a natural disaster has preserved perfectly. It is as though time has stood still, with Pompeii untouched since the day it was lost—almost 2,000 years ago.

FACT FILE

Around two-thirds of Pompeii has been uncovered. The remaining third is being left for future excavations.

◀ This mosaic was intended to warn visitors to beware of the guard dog at a Pompeii home.

▼ Around 1,500 buildings in Pompeii are being preserved by teams of archeologists.

LOST: A PREHISTORIC VILLAGE

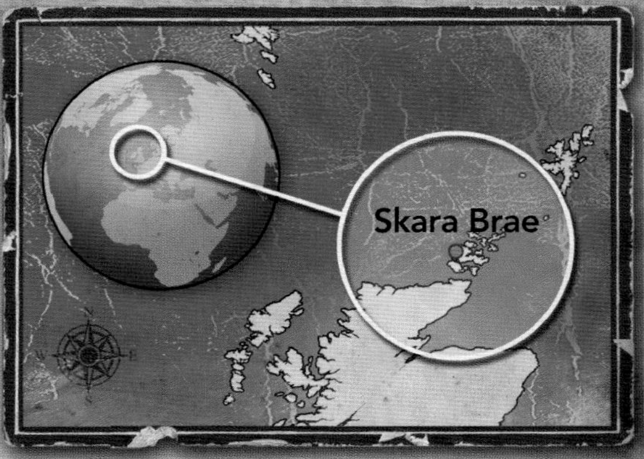

Skara Brae, Orkney Islands
Date: about 2500 BC

Thousands of years ago, a little village on the Orkney Islands off the coast of Scotland was abandoned. Between ten and twenty farming families left their homes.

Village Life

The village lay behind sand dunes, set back from the crashing waves of the Atlantic Ocean. Its stone, timber, and turf houses were built close together, with narrow, winding passageways between them. The stone house walls were very thick. Inside, flat stones paved the floors, and fires burned in open hearths.

▼ A Skara Brae family prepares a meal of seabirds and shellfish. They may have used dried seaweed for fuel.

Buried in Sand

No one knows why the village was abandoned. The sand dunes may have shifted, leaving the houses exposed to the ocean. Or a great storm may have swept the dunes over the village. All we know for sure is that the villagers left their homes. Eventually, the drifting sand completely buried the houses, and all traces of the village were lost.

▲ Skara Brae's narrow passageways can still be seen in the remains of the village. Some were roofed over, so that people had to stoop to walk along them.

Stone Furniture

Very few trees grow on the Orkney Islands, so the main building material has always been stone. It splits into flat slabs, which are perfect for stacking to make walls and pieces of furniture. The village houses had stone closets like this one. Even the beds were made of stone.

FOUND:
SKARA BRAE

▲ The Ring of Brodgar is a prehistoric circle of standing stones on another of the Orkney Islands.

In the winter of 1850, a terrible storm roared in from the Atlantic Ocean and stripped the grass off a high sand dune known as Skara Brae.

Long Lost Houses

When the storm died down, tons of sand had been blown away and stone walls stood in its place. The landowner cleared away more of the sand. He revealed more stone walls and passageways and realized he was looking at long lost houses.

In December 1924, the site was damaged when a winter storm washed away one of the ancient houses. Archeologists knew they had to act fast or the next big storm could destroy everything. Over the next few years, they uncovered all the houses. They found pieces of clayware, beads from necklaces, animal bones, and stone tools used for cutting and scraping. These objects helped them estimate the age of the village, which they said was around 4,500 years.

▲ These spoons and fork were made from the bones of seals or whales.

Strange Stones

Among the objects found at Skara Brae were four stone balls with unusual swirling carvings. They have been carefully designed and carved by a skilled craftsperson. Experts do not know whether they were religious or magical objects, or pieces of decorative art.

▼ On the ground in the center of this Skara Brae house is a hearth, where a fire would have burned.

FACT FILE

Skara Brae is the best preserved Neolithic village in northern Europe. The Neolithic Age lasted from around 4500 to 1700 BC.

LOST: AN INCA CITY

In the 1400s, the Inca people controlled a huge empire in South America. They built a fabulous estate for their emperor in present-day Peru.

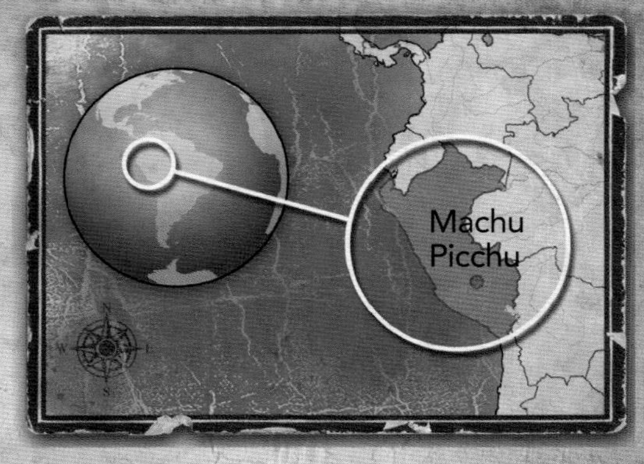

Location: Machu Picchu, Peru.
Date: 1450s

Sacred Mountains

The place chosen to build the royal estate was about a five-day walk from the Inca capital city of Cuzco. It was on a high ridge between two sacred mountains, above the Urubamba River. The estate was made up of around 140 stone buildings.

▼ The Temple of the Sun was used to honor and celebrate Inti, the Inca sun god. Twice a year, the sun shone through a window directly onto a large stone inside the temple.

Emperor Pachacuti

Pachacuti, which means "Earth Shaker," became emperor of the Incas in 1438. At the start of his 33-year reign, the Incas were a minor group of people in South America. Pachacuti created the Inca empire and made the Incas the leading people in South America.

Spanish Invasion

Emperor Pachacuti died in 1471. In 1532, Spanish invaders conquered the Inca empire. The Spanish raided many cities and towns, but they never found Machu Picchu.

There were no more Inca emperors to use the royal estate. Only around 100 years after they had built it, the defeated Incas abandoned Machu Picchu. The jungle soon closed in, and the buildings of Machu Picchu disappeared from sight.

◄ Spanish troops capture the last Inca emperor, Atahualpa. They executed him soon after, in 1533.

FOUND: MACHU PICCHU

The centuries passed, and Machu Picchu remained a secret, hidden place. Then archeologists and explorers began searching for the ruins of the Inca cities.

▲ Most of the buildings of Machu Picchu were made from stone blocks carefully cut to fit together.

Search for the Ruins

An American named Hiram Bingham thought there might be some Inca ruins in an unexplored valley of the Urubamba River. In 1911, Bingham began an expedition into the valley to look for the ruins.

After several days of trekking, a farmer told Bingham about Inca ruins high up on a steep, jungle-clad mountain. The expedition set off in search of the ruins.

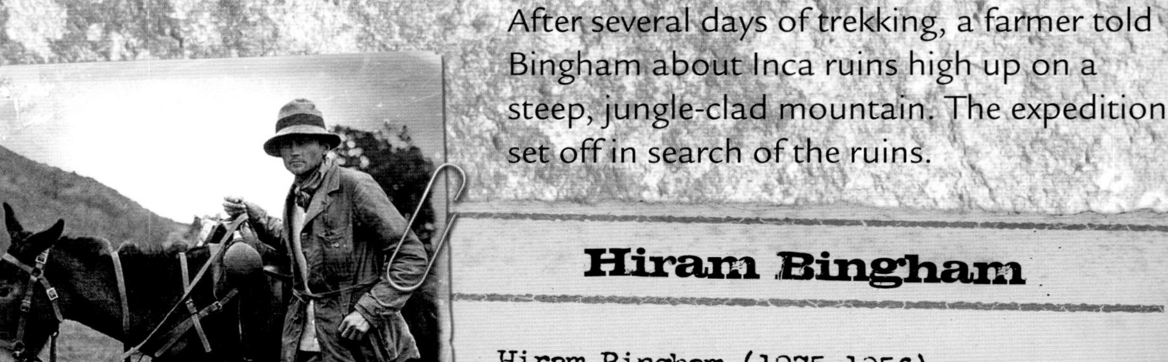

Hiram Bingham

Hiram Bingham (1875–1956) was a history teacher at Yale University in New Haven, Connecticut. When Bingham first came to Machu Picchu, he thought he had found Vilcabamba, the last stronghold of the Incas. In fact, Vilcabamba is in another valley.

Lost Inca City

To Bingham's amazement, they came upon a series of terraces, which seemed to rise up the mountain like giant steps. As he pushed his way through bamboo thickets and tangled vines, Bingham saw ruined houses, temples, and courtyards. Bingham was spellbound at the sight. As he cleared away the undergrowth and the poisonous snakes, all the buildings of Machu Picchu were revealed. Bingham called it "The Lost City of the Incas."

FACT FILE

Experts think that most of the people who lived at Machu Picchu died of smallpox, caught from foreign travelers.

▼ Machu Picchu is almost 8,000 feet (2,400 meters) above sea level—high enough to make some people sick from lack of oxygen.

WHAT IS TREASURE?

Whether it is sparkling gold and jewels or a collection of dusty old scrolls, all treasure is valuable. There is something magical about treasure, because it has a story to tell about the past.

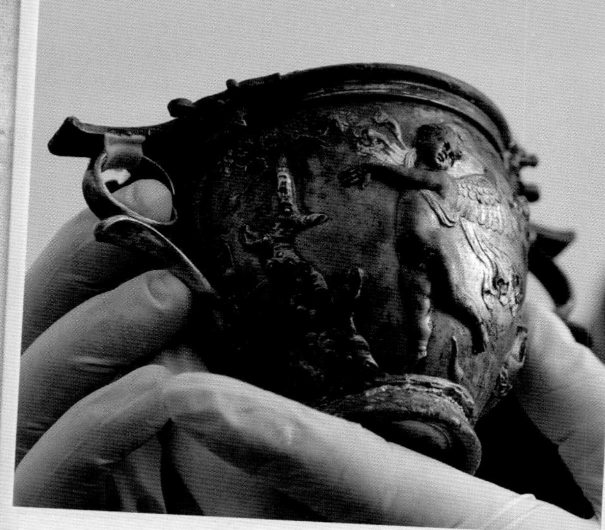

▲ In 2009, archeologists in Bulgaria found this 2,000-year-old silver cup, decorated with figures from Greek mythology.

Hidden or Lost

Valuable things become lost treasure for different reasons. Sometimes people hide their precious possessions and are not able to return to them. Ships carrying valuable cargo can sink on their journeys. Other treasures are buried in graves.

◀ The ship carrying this Ancient Greek figure of a warrior to Italy sank. It stayed on the seabed until 1972, when it was found by a diver.

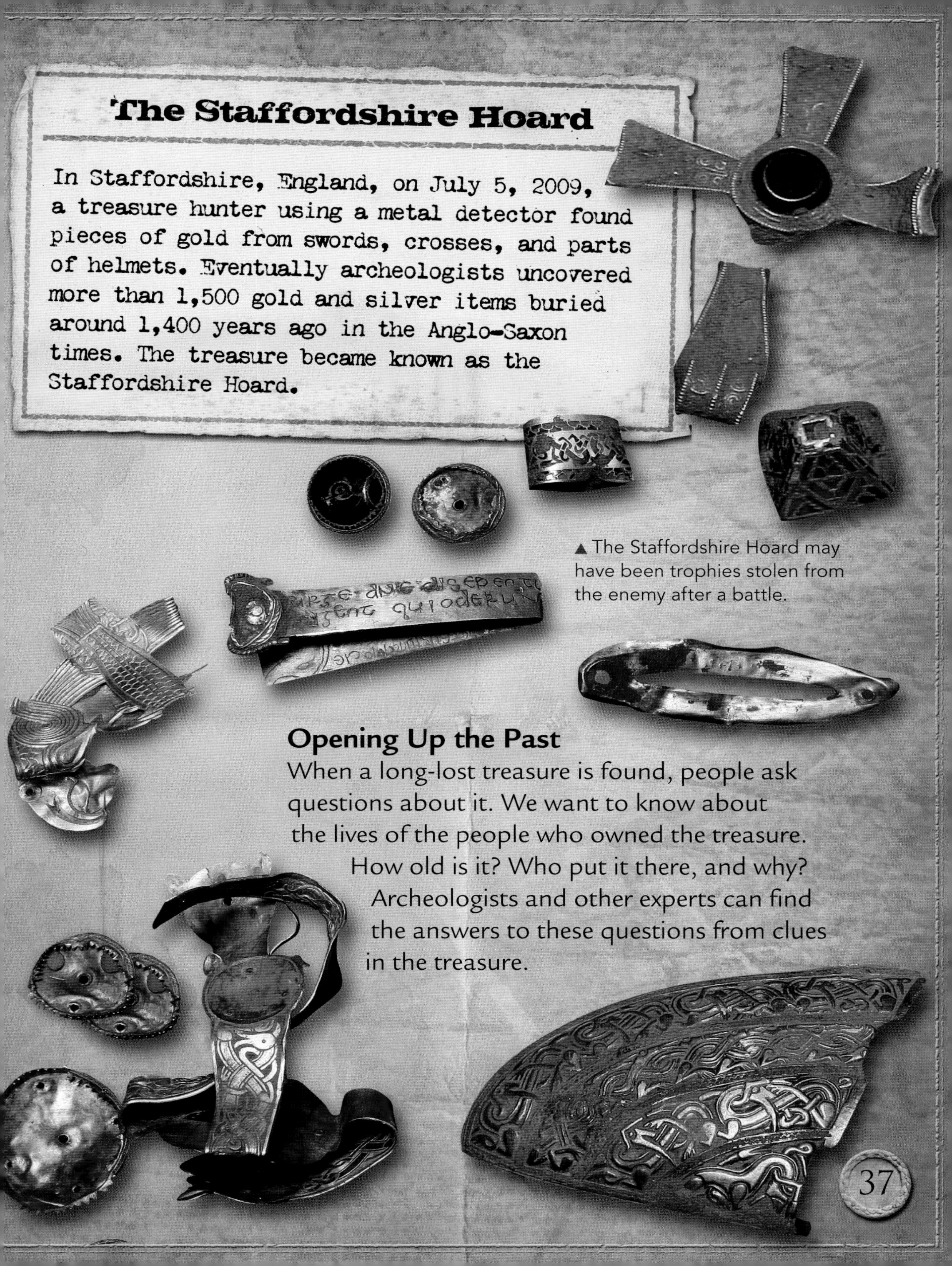

The Staffordshire Hoard

In Staffordshire, England, on July 5, 2009, a treasure hunter using a metal detector found pieces of gold from swords, crosses, and parts of helmets. Eventually archeologists uncovered more than 1,500 gold and silver items buried around 1,400 years ago in the Anglo-Saxon times. The treasure became known as the Staffordshire Hoard.

▲ The Staffordshire Hoard may have been trophies stolen from the enemy after a battle.

Opening Up the Past

When a long-lost treasure is found, people ask questions about it. We want to know about the lives of the people who owned the treasure. How old is it? Who put it there, and why? Archeologists and other experts can find the answers to these questions from clues in the treasure.

LOST: ALL THE EMPEROR'S MEN

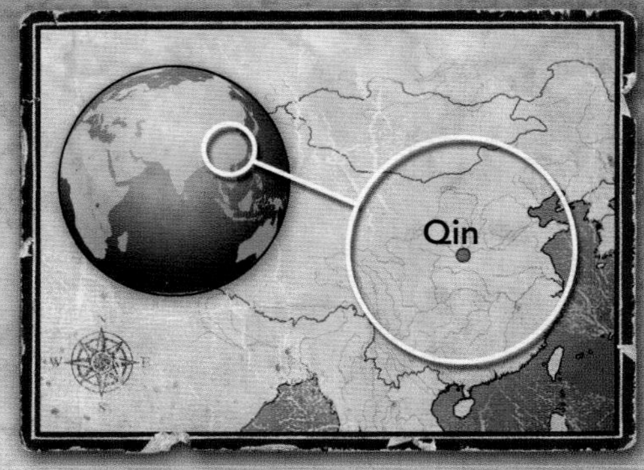

Location: Near Xi'an, eastern China
Date: 210 BC

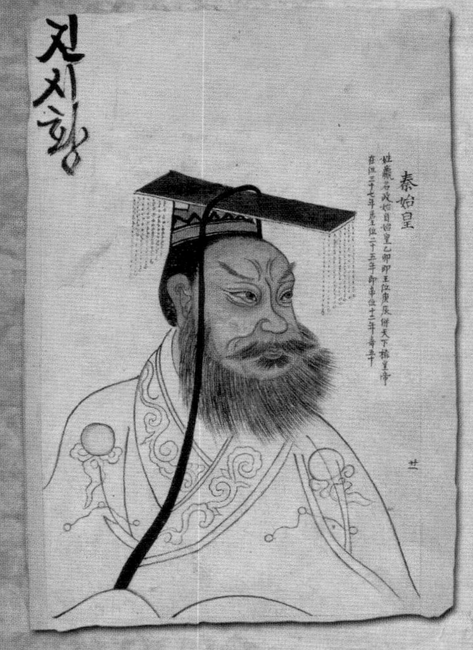

▲ When Emperor Qin died in 210 BC, he was only 50 years old.

The first Emperor of China, Qin Shi Huang, controlled the whole of China and its millions of people. To protect his vast empire, he built the Great Wall of China.

To Live Forever

But Emperor Qin wanted more than this—he wanted to live forever. His doctors gave him a substance called mercury to make him live longer. In fact, it slowly poisoned him. Years before his death, Emperor Qin had chosen his burial place. For 40 years, 700,000 men worked to make an underground tomb for him where he would be able to realize his dream and live forever.

▲ The life-size warriors stood in lines. They had their backs to the Emperor so they were ready to face any enemies.

Inside the Tomb

The Emperor's tomb contained everything he would need for eternal life—animals, chariots and horses, armor and helmets, and clayware figures of entertainers and court officials. Three enormous pits contained the Emperor's army of more than 8,000 men made of terracotta, or baked clay.

◄ A huge artificial hill covered the tomb. Inside, the workers had dug out more than 600 pits as well as other tombs.

Model Warriors

Every terracotta warrior was different. They may have been modeled on real soldiers from Emperor Qin's army. Workers fixed the ears, nose, and hair on the model, then shaped the mouth, eyes, beard, and mustache onto the head.

FOUND: THE TERRACOTTA ARMY

In March 1974, some local Chinese farmers began to drill wells, but instead of water they found pieces of broken clayware and old weapons. What were they, and what were they doing there?

▲ When the Chinese farmers found the army, it looked like a jigsaw of broken pieces of clayware.

An Army of Clay

Soon, archeologists were making one of their greatest discoveries. They found an army of life-size figures in huge pits beneath the ground. The figures were made of terracotta, and soon became known as the Terracotta Army.

For 2,200 years, this army of clay had guarded Emperor Qin's tomb. But now, many of the warriors were broken into tiny pieces.

▶ Archeologists put each warrior back together, piece by piece.

FACT FILE

Each warrior took around 150 days to make, from shaping the clay into a figure to painting the warrior.

▲ Chinese restorers are planning to repaint the figures in their original bright colors.

The Emperor's Tomb

The place where Emperor Qin is buried is around 1 mile (1.5 kilometers) from the Terracotta Army. Archeologists are not yet ready to explore the tomb, but they have found traces of mercury in the earth, so the tomb may contain the rivers of mercury the emperor believed would make him live forever.

LOST: A LIBRARY OF SCROLLS

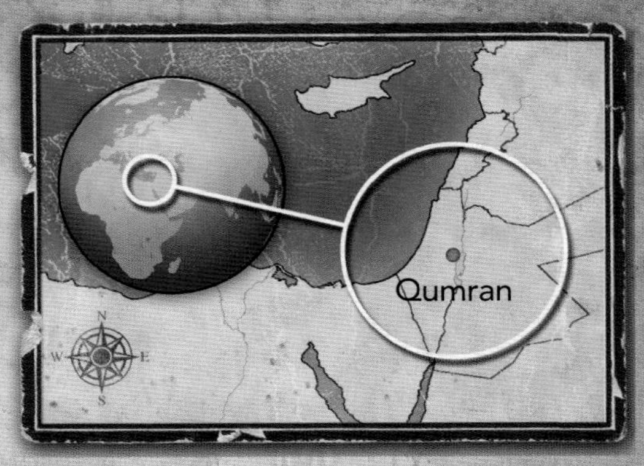

Location: Qumran, West Bank (Palestine)
Date: 66–70 AD

The Essenes were a group of deeply religious male Jews who had chosen to live in the wilderness. They were dedicated to making and looking after their library.

Making Books

Inside a special building called a scriptorium, the men copied old holy texts onto rolls of paper-like material called scrolls. They also made scrolls about their own beliefs. Copying by hand was the only way of making new texts for future generations to read. The scrolls were the Essenes' most precious possessions, and they would do anything to protect them.

▶ The scriptorium was the most important building for the Essenes' community at Qumran.

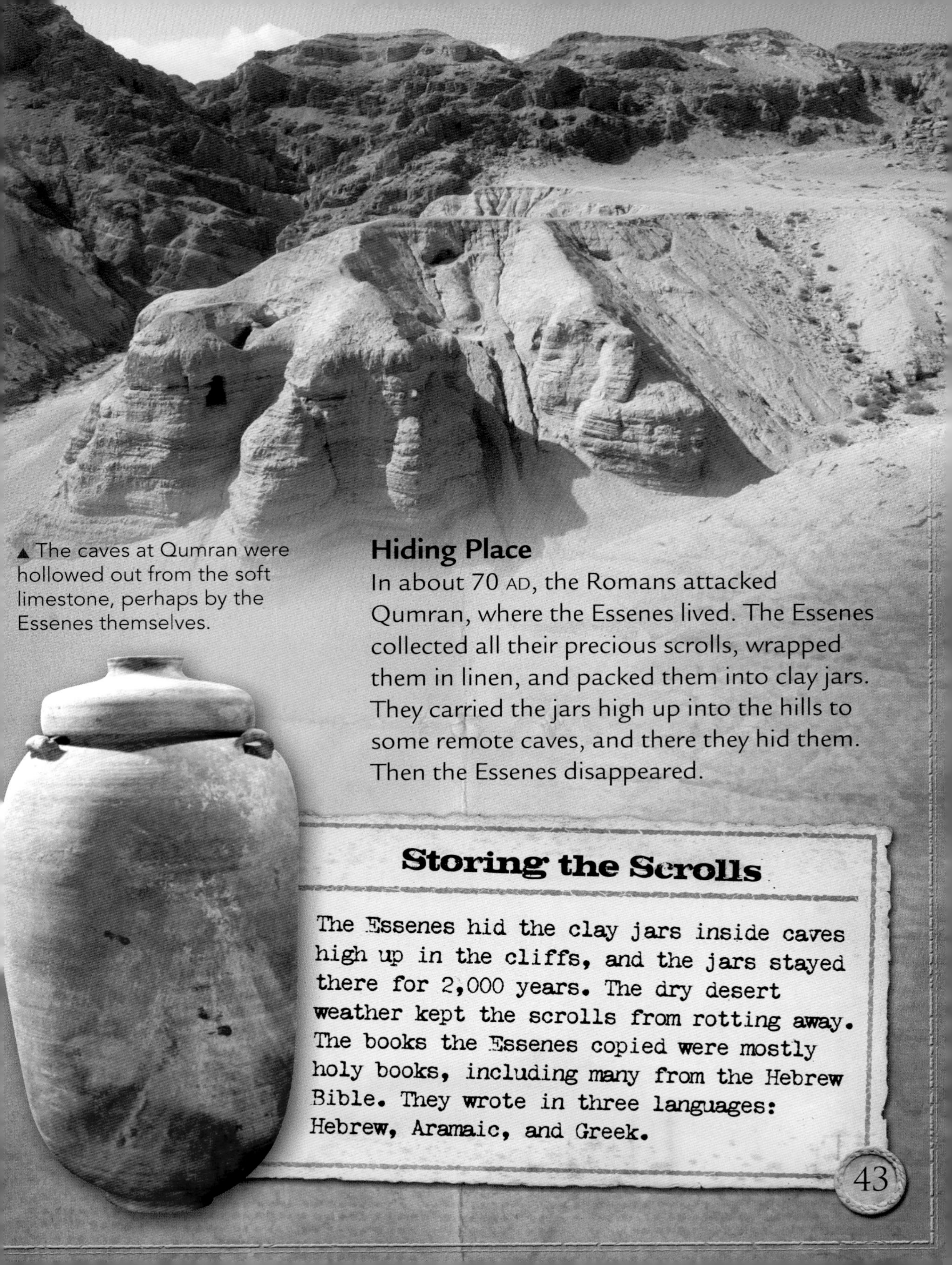

▲ The caves at Qumran were hollowed out from the soft limestone, perhaps by the Essenes themselves.

Hiding Place

In about 70 AD, the Romans attacked Qumran, where the Essenes lived. The Essenes collected all their precious scrolls, wrapped them in linen, and packed them into clay jars. They carried the jars high up into the hills to some remote caves, and there they hid them. Then the Essenes disappeared.

Storing the Scrolls

The Essenes hid the clay jars inside caves high up in the cliffs, and the jars stayed there for 2,000 years. The dry desert weather kept the scrolls from rotting away. The books the Essenes copied were mostly holy books, including many from the Hebrew Bible. They wrote in three languages: Hebrew, Aramaic, and Greek.

FOUND:
THE DEAD SEA SCROLLS

FACT FILE

The Temple Scroll is the longest of all the Dead Sea Scrolls. It is more than 25 feet (8 meters) long.

It was the winter of 1946 to 1947 in Qumran, a remote, rocky place. A young shepherd boy, Mohammed Ahmed el-Hamed, wandered into one of the caves looking for his lost goat.

▶ Archeologists search the Qumran area. They found the Essenes' settlement as well as the scrolls.

Secret Cave

According to one story, Mohammed threw a stone into the darkness, then heard a crack as it smashed something. Mohammed was curious. He fetched his cousin, and the two boys began to explore the cave.

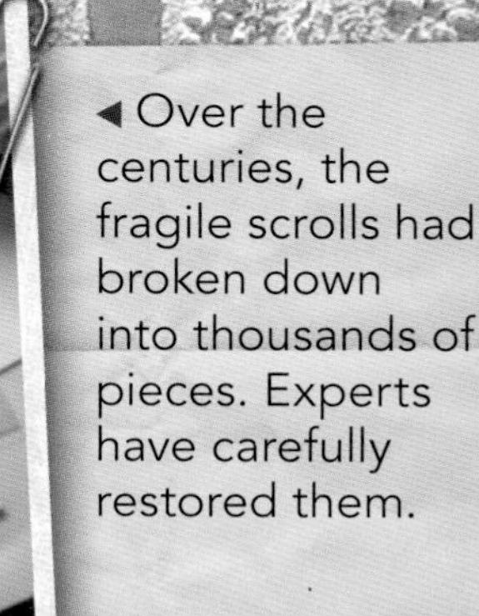

◀ Over the centuries, the fragile scrolls had broken down into thousands of pieces. Experts have carefully restored them.

World News

The boys soon found a pottery jar, broken to pieces by Mohammed's stone. The jar's contents—bundles of linen—were scattered around, and inside were dusty old scrolls.

When archeologists heard about the discovery, they went to investigate. Eventually, they found around 900 ancient scrolls hidden in 11 caves. After almost 2,000 years, the lost library of the Essenes had been found. The discovery of the Dead Sea Scrolls made news headlines around the world. It is the oldest and most complete collection of Biblical texts to have survived from ancient times.

Making Scrolls

The Essenes wrote on sections of parchment or papyrus, in ink, from right to left. When one section was full of writing, they joined a new section to the end and continued writing. When they reached the end of a story, they rolled up the sections into a scroll. So each scroll was a complete text, just like a book.

LOST:
GOLD IN THE LAKE

In Colombia, South America, lies Lake Guatavita. The Muisca people believed that a goddess called Chie lived in the lake. To keep her happy, they had to give Chie gifts of precious things.

Location: Lake Guatavita, Colombia
Date: 1500s

Before the Ceremony

The gift-giving ceremony for the goddess of the lake was a new king's first duty. To prepare for the ceremony, he had to spend several days alone in a cave, allowed out only at nighttime. The new king was also forbidden eating salt or chili pepper—the Muisca people believed this would make his body pure.

▼ Lake Guatavita is an almost perfect circle and about 120 feet (37 meters) deep.

The Gold Raft

This is a gold model of the king and his chiefs on the raft that floated across Lake Guatavita. Over the years, thousands of jewels and gold items were thrown into the lake by the king, his chiefs, and worshipers on the shore. They sank to the bottom of the lake, and the Muisca people forgot all about them.

Golden Man

After the purification, servants took the king to Lake Guatavita. There they stripped him naked and smeared his body with mud. They blew gold dust over him, which stuck to the mud. The gold dust covered him from top to toe, turning him into a golden man.

Then the king and four of his chiefs stood on a raft. The raft floated to the center of the lake, where they threw handfuls of gold objects and emeralds into the water.

▼ Attendants blew gold dust through reed pipes onto the king's body.

FOUND:
THE GOLD OF EL DORADO

In the 1530s, explorers from Spain arrived in Colombia in search of gold. They had heard stories about a mountain kingdom where gold was commonplace.

▲ This figure of a warrior god is made from pure gold. In one hand he holds an enemy's head, and in the other a knife.

El Dorado

The Spanish explorers called the mysterious kingdom El Dorado, which means "the golden one." In the 1540s, they became convinced that Lake Guatavita was the site of El Dorado, and they were determined to reveal all its treasures. They made local people carry away buckets of water day after day until the muddy edges of the lake were exposed, but only a few pieces of gold were revealed.

The search of Lake Guatavita continued until, in 1965, the Colombian government banned further searches. And so the story ends, perhaps with untold riches still at the center of Lake Guatavita.

Precious Metal

To the Muisca people, gold was a beautiful metal to make sacred objects with, such as this figure. To the Spanish, gold meant wealth. Some of them were determined to get as much as they could, even if that meant stealing it.

▼ The Spanish searched South America for a golden kingdom they called El Dorado.

FACT FILE

Experts have estimated that half a million offerings were thrown into Lake Guatavita.

▼ This gold headpiece is decorated with two big circles that look like the eyes of a jungle cat.

WHAT IS A LOST SHIP?

The seabed is littered with the wrecks of tens of thousands of ships. Every one of them has a story to tell about a voyage that ended in disaster.

▲ A marine archeologist surveys the site of an ancient wreck off the coast of Italy.

Reasons for Wrecks

There are many reasons why ships become lost at sea. Weather is the greatest danger. Storms have caused many shipwrecks. Sometimes sailors steer their ships too close to rocks or other ships and cause a collision. Piracy is a real danger, too. And in wartime, ships can be sunk when under attack from enemy fire.

▼ This is a reconstruction of the Uluburun ship, wrecked off the coast of Turkey 3,300 years ago.

◀ Ships called galleys were used in warfare from ancient times to the 1500s and were often wrecked.

Recovering Objects

When a lost ship is found, the experts can begin to recover objects from it and bring them back up into the daylight for everyone to see. In some special cases, even the ship itself is brought ashore and put on display in a museum.

The Kyrenia Ship

The wreck of an ancient Greek merchant ship from the 300s BC was discovered off Kyrenia, Cyprus, in 1965. The ship's wooden hull, shown here, was raised. Archeologists determined that the Kyrenia ship had been transporting wine and almonds in large clayware jars called amphorae between the Greek islands.

LOST: LUXURY LINER

On April 10, 1912, the largest and most luxurious passenger liner ever built set sail from Southampton, England. The ship's name was the *Titanic*.

Location: North Atlantic Ocean
Date: April 14, 1912

▼ These second-class passengers expected to enjoy a luxury that only a first-class ticket would buy on other ocean liners.

Passengers' Hopes

Onboard the *Titanic* were a crew of 899 and 1,324 passengers. Most passengers were poor people traveling third class—the cheapest tickets. They were emigrants, who had dreams of starting new lives in the U.S.A. It was not to be.

Close to midnight on Sunday, April 14, a lookout shouted: "Iceberg, right ahead!" The collision could not be avoided. The liner's side scraped against the iceberg, splitting open her hull below the waterline.

▶ Queenstown, Ireland was the liner's last stop before she sailed out into the Atlantic Ocean.

An Unsinkable Ship?

As the *Titanic* was being built, she was described as "virtually unsinkable" by her shipbuilders, Harland and Wolff. But a rumor spread that the *Titanic* really was unsinkable. In reality, the ship was not completely watertight. When water entered the hull, it poured through gaps, and the *Titanic* was doomed.

Fateful Night

Nothing could stop the freezing water from pouring through the hull, or save the *Titanic* from sinking to the bottom of the North Atlantic Ocean. Of the 2,223 people that sailed on the *Titanic*, 1,517 drowned or died of cold in the icy water.

▼ The fortunate survivors watch the *Titanic* plunge to the seabed.

FOUND: THE *TITANIC*

FACT FILE

Nearly 6,000 artifacts have been raised from the *Titanic*. They are on display in museums, and are not allowed to be sold.

A few years after the *Titanic* sank, people began to talk about finding her wreck. But it was 70 years before a serious search to find the ship began.

The Search

The *Titanic* sank around 500 miles (800 kilometers) off the coast of Newfoundland, in Canada. In the 1980s, a U.S. explorer named Jack Grimm tried to find the wreck three times, but he failed. Someone else who dreamed of finding the *Titanic* was U.S. marine geologist (scientist of the ocean floor) Robert Ballard. He had spent years exploring the oceans with underwater vehicles.

First Sightings

In 1985, Ballard began to search the North Atlantic seabed with underwater vehicles, looking for the lost liner. From the control room of his ship, Ballard operated a tiny underwater vehicle called *Argo*. For five weeks, *Argo* found nothing. Then it filmed a large metal object on the seabed. Ballard looked closely and realized the pictures showed a ship's boiler. Next, he saw the unmistakable shape of a ship on his screen. It was the *Titanic*.

▼ Anchor chains on the deck of the *Titanic*, photographed in 2003.

Amazing Argo

The *Titanic* was found by *Argo*, a remotely operated vehicle (R.O.V.). *Argo* was lowered into the water by a crane on the surface ship. The ship pulled *Argo* behind it. *Argo* was fitted with video cameras that sent pictures back up to the main ship. Its powerful headlights lit up the dark ocean

LOST: THE KING'S FLAGSHIP

On a summer's day in 1545, a simple mistake caused a Tudor warship to sink close to the shore. Her name was the *Mary Rose*, and she was King Henry VIII's flagship.

Location: Off Portsmouth, England
Date: July 19, 1545

▼ Armed with 91 guns, the *Mary Rose* was the pride of the English fleet.

Preparing for Battle

In 1545, the *Mary Rose* led a fleet of about 80 ships out of Portsmouth harbor. They were ready to battle an invading French fleet.

King Henry VIII

Henry VIII is one of England's best-known monarchs and a member of the Tudor dynasty. Henry ruled for 38 years (from 1509 to 1547) and is most famous for having six wives and for changing England from a Catholic to a Protestant country. He also built a powerful navy.

Disaster Unfolds

The *Mary Rose* fired its guns on one side at an enemy ship when it was caught by a strong gust of wind. As her sails filled, the *Mary Rose* leaned over, the open gunports dipped below the surface of the sea, and water rushed in. The *Mary Rose* capsized, taking around 400 men to a watery grave. Standing on the shore was King Henry VIII, watching in horror at the disaster.

▼ Horrified sailors battle against the torrent of water gushing onto the deck of the *Mary Rose*.

FOUND: THE *MARY ROSE*

FACT FILE

Only the right (starboard) side of the *Mary Rose* has survived. The left (port) side has rotted away.

Soon after she sank in 1545, an attempt was made to lift the *Mary Rose*, but all that was raised were some cannons.

Left on the Seabed

Time passed, and the Tudor warship sank deep into the muddy seabed. Shipworms ate through her oak timbers, and powerful ocean currents pushed and pulled at her, breaking her open. Ships passed over her as they sailed to and from Portsmouth harbor. Then, in 1971, an amateur diver found the *Mary Rose* once again.

▲ These gold coins, found on the *Mary Rose*, are known as "angels" because of their design.

▲ This set of wooden knives (right) and bone lice comb (left) are among the objects found on the *Mary Rose*.

Mary Rose Raised

A team of marine archeologists spent the next 11 years uncovering the "Tudor time capsule." They recovered almost 20,000 objects from the wreck and the bones of hundreds of sailors who had drowned in the tragedy. In 1982, the *Mary Rose* herself was raised. She was taken to Portsmouth—the port she had left 437 years earlier, where she went on display in a museum built specially for her.

▼ The hull of the *Mary Rose* was raised inside a metal cradle by a giant crane.

Preserving the *Mary Rose*

After 437 years underwater, the timbers of the *Mary Rose*'s hull were waterlogged. If they dried out, they would shrink and crack. From 1982 to 2004, experts worked to preserve the hull. They used a special chemical to squeeze out the water and replace it with wax.

LOST: CIVIL WAR SUBMARINE

From 1861 to 1865, the U.S.A. fought a bitter civil war. As often happens in wars, new weapons were invented. During the American Civil War, the first submarine was used in warfare.

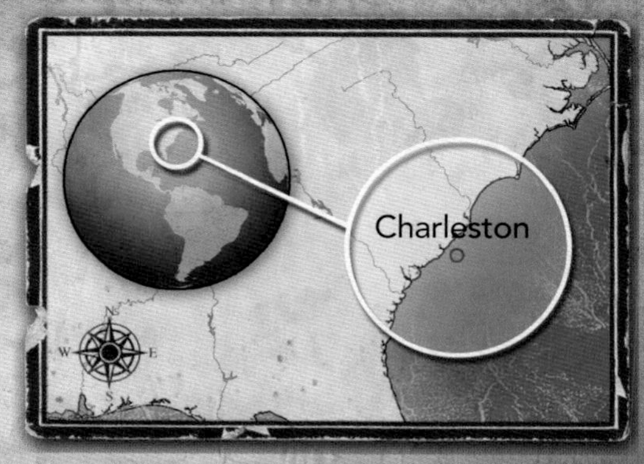

Location: Off Charleston, South Carolina
Date: February 17, 1864

True Submersible

The submarine was named *H.L. Hunley* after its designer and captain. She was a true submersible, able to dive and travel underwater, then return to the surface. The *Hunley* was 40 feet (12 meters) long and was crewed by eight brave submariners. Seven of them made the propeller spin around, and the eighth man steered.

▼ Artist Conrad Chapman made this painting of the *Hunley* in 1863 when the submarine was in the dockyard at Charleston, South Carolina.

Mission to Sink *Housatonic*

On February 17, 1864, the *Hunley* went on her one and only mission—to sink the *U.S.S. Housatonic*. She was armed with a torpedo packed with about 100 pounds (45 kilograms) of gunpowder. The crew fixed the torpedo to the *Housatonic*'s hull, then detonated it by pulling a cord—from a safe distance. The torpedo exploded, sinking the *Housatonic* as planned. It was the first time a submarine had been used to sink an enemy ship. But something went very wrong, and the *Hunley* sank, too, taking the crew with her.

▲ This artist's impression shows the *Hunley* on her mission to sink the *Housatonic*. She carries a single torpedo mounted on a long spear.

Ironclads

The American Civil War also saw the first "ironclads." These steam-powered ships made of iron were the world's first modern battleships. This is the *C.S.S. Virginia*, an ironclad of the Confederate States Navy. In 1862, she fought the United States Navy ironclad, the *U.S.S. Monitor*, in the first battle between ironclads.

FOUND:
H.L. HUNLEY

For 100 years, no one knew where the wreck of the *Hunley* was—until Edward Lee Spence went on a fishing trip off Charleston, South Carolina.

Trapped Line

Spence plunged into the cold water to free a trapped line. As he tugged at the line, he saw it was snagged on a long, smooth metal object. Spence knew about the *Hunley* submarine, and as he broke the surface, he called out: "I've found the *Hunley*!"

▼ At a conservation center in Charleston, part of the *Hunley's* hull was removed, allowing marine archeologists to work inside the submarine.

Submarine Uncovered

Twenty-five years after the wreck had been found, an expedition to raise the *Hunley* began. The submarine was partly covered by a thick layer of sand, but underwater vacuum cleaners carefully sucked it away, and little by little the *Hunley* was uncovered. On August 8, 2000, the lost submarine was gently raised back to the surface. Onboard were the remains of the eight submariners who had lost their lives way back in 1864.

FACT FILE

The *Hunley* sank in only around 27 feet (8.2 meters) of water, just beyond the entrance to Charleston Harbor.

◀ This leather purse belonged to one of the crew of the *Hunley*.

Lucky Gold Coin

This $20 gold coin belonged to the *Hunley*'s commander, Lieutenant George E. Dixon. He had fought in the Civil War's Battle of Shiloh, and the coin had saved his life when a bullet bounced off it. For a lucky charm, Dixon had the coin engraved with the words "Shiloh April 6th 1862 My Life Preserver G.E.D."

INDEX